Fish Community Monitoring at Hot Springs National Park

2009 Report

Natural Resource Report NPS/HTLN/NRDS—2012/235

Hope R. Dodd

National Park Service
Heartland I&M Network
Wilson's Creek National Battlefield
6424 W Farm Road 182
Republic, MO 65738

Samantha K. Mueller

University of Minnesota Duluth
Biology
207 SSB
1035 Kirby Drive
Duluth, MN 55812

February 2012

U.S. Department of the Interior
National Park Service
Natural Resource Stewardship and Science
Fort Collins, Colorado

The National Park Service, Natural Resource Stewardship and Science office in Fort Collins, Colorado publishes a range of reports that address natural resource topics of interest and applicability to a broad audience in the National Park Service and others in natural resource management, including scientists, conservation and environmental constituencies, and the public.

The Natural Resource Data Series is intended for the timely release of basic data sets and data summaries. Care has been taken to assure accuracy of raw data values, but a thorough analysis and interpretation of the data has not been completed. Consequently, the initial analyses of data in this report are provisional and subject to change.

All manuscripts in the series receive the appropriate level of peer review to ensure that the information is scientifically credible, technically accurate, appropriately written for the intended audience, and designed and published in a professional manner.

This report received informal peer review by subject-matter experts who were not directly involved in the collection, analysis, or reporting of the data. Data in this report were collected and analyzed using methods based on established, peer-reviewed protocols and were analyzed and interpreted within the guidelines of the protocols.

Views, statements, findings, conclusions, recommendations, and data in this report do not necessarily reflect views and policies of the National Park Service, U.S. Department of the Interior. Mention of trade names or commercial products does not constitute endorsement or recommendation for use by the U.S. Government.

This report is available from the Heartland Inventory and Monitoring website (http://science.nature.nps.gov/im/units/htln/) and the Natural Resource Publications Management website (http://www.nature.nps.gov/publications/nrpm/).

Please cite this publication as:

Dodd, H. R. and S. K. Mueller. 2011. Fish community monitoring at Hot Springs National Park: 2009 report. Natural Resource Data Series NPS/HTLN/NRDS—2012/235. National Park Service, Fort Collins, Colorado.

NPS 128/112671, February 2012

Contents

Figures

Tables

Abstract

In June 2009, the Heartland Inventory and Monitoring Network of the National Park Service began monitoring water quality and fish communities in Gulpha Creek and Bull Bayou to collect baseline data and assess the status of these aquatic resources. Fish were collected in a single pass with a backpack electrofishing unit in one 150 m reach of each stream. Physical habitat data were collected using an 11 transect method. Water quality data were recorded using data loggers over a 2-day period. Bull Bayou had more than twice as many species of fish as Gulpha Creek (17 compared to 7), but overall diversity was the same for both streams (Simpson's Index = 0.20 for both). Stream integrity was rated as good for Bull Bayou (IBI = 28) and fair for Gulpha Creek (IBI = 20). Both streams had sensitive species present, but Bull Bayou had a higher number of intolerant species than Gulpha Creek and fewer incidences of fish disease or anomalies. Water quality parameters were within the standards set by the Arkansas Pollution Control and Ecology Commission (APCEC 2010). In-stream habitat conditions and bank stability were favorable for supporting a native fish community typical of wadeable Ouachita Mountain streams.

Acknowledgments

Thanks to J. Tyler Cribbs, Myranda Clark, Rachael Heth and Ann Kjellerson for assistance with field work. We would also like to acknowledge Steve Rudd at HOSP for his helpful advice and support.

Introduction

Hot Springs National Park (HOSP), located in the Ouachita Mountains Ecoregion of Arkansas, was established to preserve the geothermal springs and conserve this water resource for public use. The park is 22.5 km^2 and, in addition to the hot springs, contains portions of three streams: Gulpha Creek (3.1 km), Bull Bayou (1.9 km), and Whittington Creek (2.3 km). Land use adjacent to the park is primarily urban, with the park surrounding the north end of the city of Hot Springs, Arkansas. Urbanization can have a negative impact on the quality of surface water and adversely affect fish populations through habitat loss and fragmentation, sedimentation, and non-point source water pollution. In June 2009, the Heartland Inventory and Monitoring Network (HTLN) of the National Park Service (NPS) began monitoring water quality and fish communities in Gulpha Creek and Bull Bayou to assess the integrity of these surface water resources. Whittington Creek, an intermittent stream, was not monitored.

Fish communities are an important component of stream systems and are useful biological indicators of aquatic ecosystem health. Changes or shifts in stream habitat complexity and water quality often determine biotic communities, including fish (Lazorchak et al. 1998). Many fish species are considered intolerant of habitat alterations and poor water quality (Robison and Buchanan 1988; Pflieger 1997; Barbour et al. 1999). Historically, trends in the composition and abundance of fish populations have been used to assess the biological integrity of streams (Karr 1981; Barbour et al. 1999; Moulton et al. 2002). Therefore, monitoring fish community composition along with associated water quality and habitat conditions serves as a strong basis for measuring stream integrity. Moreover, the intrinsic value of fish to the public as environmental indicators and as a recreational opportunity makes the status of fish diversity a valuable interpretive topic for the park visitor and an informative tool for protecting and conserving the surface water resources at HOSP.

Objectives of fish community monitoring at HOSP are: (1) to determine the status and long-term trends in fish richness, diversity, abundance, and community composition and (2) to correlate the long-term community data to overall water quality and habitat condition.

Methods

Details on methods of site selection, fish sampling, and habitat and water quality data collection not listed in this report can be found in the Protocol for Monitoring Fish Communities in Small Streams in the Heartland Inventory and Monitoring Network (Dodd et al. 2008).

Study Area and Site Selection

A reach on Gulpha Creek and a reach on Bull Bayou were selected within the park boundaries (Figure 1). Reach length was defined as 20 times the mean wetted stream width (MWSW) with a minimum of 150 m, allowing inclusion of representative channel units (riffle, run, and pool habitats) located within the stream (Moulton et al. 2002). Because the streams at HOSP were small and narrow, the minimum reach length of 150 m was sampled.

Fish Collection

Fish communities were sampled in June of 2009. Fish were collected using a single pass with a pulsed DC backpack electrofishing unit throughout the sampling reach. During sampling, fish were collected with nets and placed in aerated buckets. All fish were identified to species, if possible, and counted; and a subsample of 30 individuals per species were inspected for anomalies (deformities, eroded fins, lesions, tumors, and blackspot parasite). Fish that were too small or that were difficult to identify in the field were preserved for laboratory identification. All other fish were released back into the sample reach. Details on fish collection and sample processing techniques can be found in Dodd et al. (2008) (see SOP #4).

Habitat and Water Quality

Physical habitat and water quality data were collected in conjunction with fish sampling. An 11 transect method was used to collect data on general channel morphology, fish cover, and bank conditions within the entire reach. In-stream habitat (depth, velocity, substrate, *etc.*) and fish cover (presence of boulders, hydrophytes, *etc.*) were assessed at three points per transect (see Dodd et al. (2008), SOP #5 for a list of all habitat parameters collected). Fish cover along the banks (undercut banks, overhanging terrestrial vegetation, *etc.*) and bank/riparian stability were assessed on the left and right banks at each transect. Hourly water quality data (temperature, dissolved oxygen, pH, specific conductance, and turbidity) were collected using a logger deployed upstream of each reach for two days. Detailed methods on habitat and water quality collection are located in Dodd et al. (2008) (see SOP #3 and #5).

Data Analysis

Biological metrics that reflect fish community diversity (species richness and Simpson's Diversity Index), abundance (catch per unit effort), composition (number and percent composition of sensitive taxa), and overall stream integrity (Index of Biotic Integrity) were calculated. Community diversity was assessed using Simpson's Diversity Index which gives the probability that two individuals picked at random from the site are the same species. Therefore, the index decreases with increasing diversity and ranges from 0 (completely diverse) to 1 (no diversity). For community composition, number and percent composition of sucker (Catastomidae), sunfish (Centrarchidae), and darter/sculpin/madtom (*Etheostoma* and *Percina/Cottus/Noturus*) species were calculated because these metrics are typically used in several Index of Biotic Integrity (IBI) calculations (Karr 1981, Hlass et al. 1998, Dauwalter et al. 2003, Smogor 2005) and demonstrate sensitivity to human disturbance. The IBI developed by

Hlass et al. (1998) was used to assess overall stream health and includes eight metrics: 1) number of fish species; 2) number and identity of Cyprinidae species; 3) number of sensitive species; 4) percent of individuals as Green sunfish (*Lepomis cyanellus*); 5) ratio of generalist to specialist feeders; 6) percent of individuals as top carnivores; 7) number of individuals in sample; 8) percent of individuals with disease or anomaly (eroded fins, lesions, tumor or blackspot parasite). Scoring criteria was used (1 = worst, 3 = moderate, 5 = best) for each of the eight raw metric values. The metric scores were added to calculate an IBI score that ranges from 8 (poor) to 40 (excellent).

Physical habitat and water quality data were summarized using averages with standard errors (SE) or percentages, where appropriate. Physical habitat data were analyzed as in-stream habitat, fish cover, and bank stability. Analysis of in-stream substrate data used the Wentworth code for particle sizes (see SOP #5 in Dodd et al. 2008 for the code categories and size ranges). For assessment of stream banks, categories of bank angle, percent vegetation, height, and substrate were used to assess overall bank stability. Water quality data are presented as averages and standard errors.

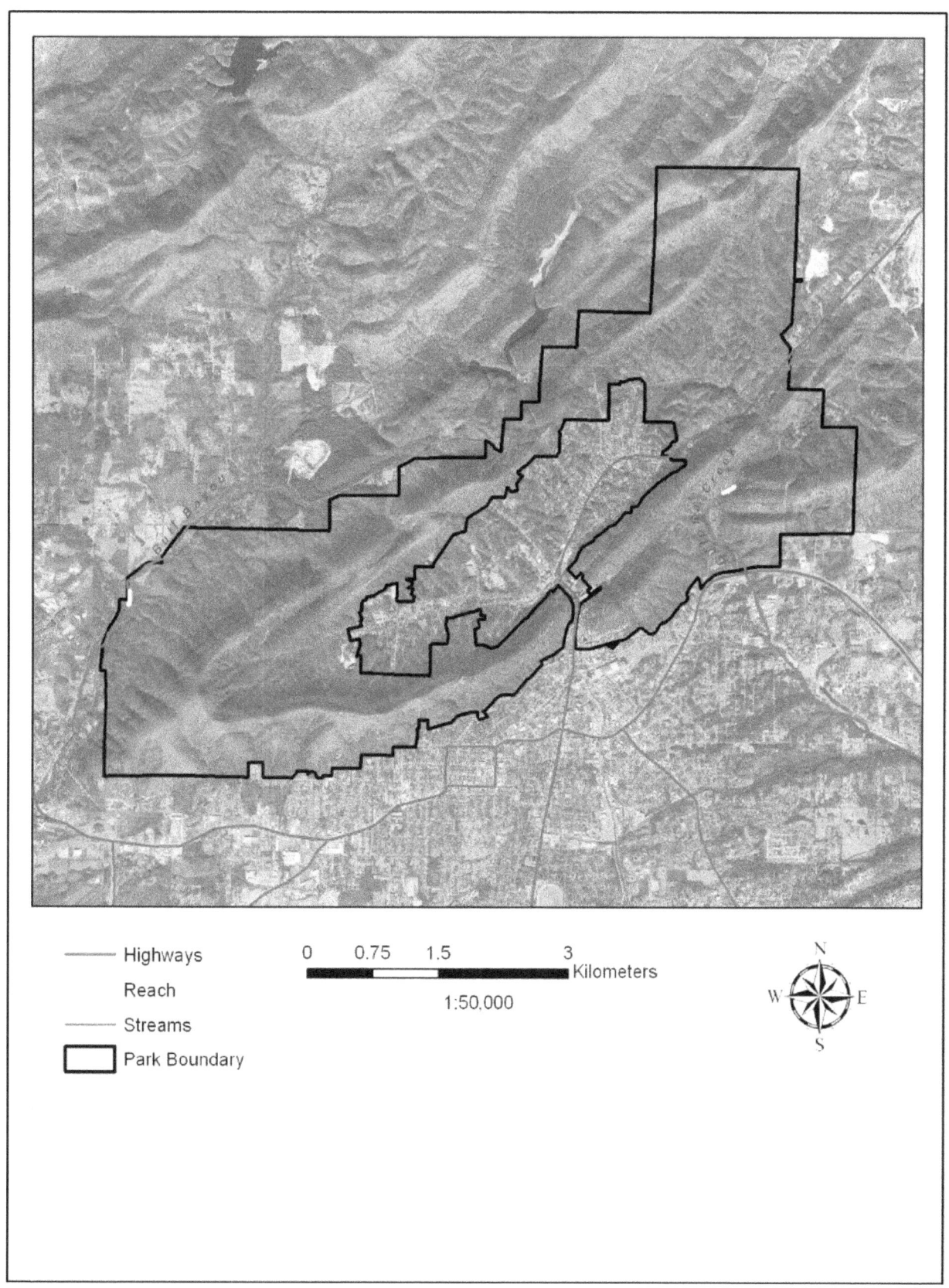

Highways
Reach
Streams
Park Boundary

0   0.75   1.5   3
Kilometers
1:50,000

Figure 1. Fish monitoring reach locations in Gulpha Creek and Bull Bayou.

Results

Fish Community

Eighteen fish species were collected at HOSP with Bull Bayou having more than twice as many species as Gulpha Creek (Tables 1 and 2). Diversity was high in both streams (low Simpson's Index of 0.20), but total abundance of fish was low (Table 1). The community in Gulpha Creek consisted primarily of minnow species (Cyprinidae; 49.3%) of which one species, the Striped shiner (*Luxilus chrysocephalus*), is considered intolerant to poor water quality (Tables 1 and 2). Twenty nine percent of the fish community consisted of the Orangebelly darter (*Etheostoma radiosum*), another species sensitive to human disturbance that requires clean gravel/cobble substrate. Of the 17 species collected in Bull Bayou, five species are intolerant to poor water quality and habitat conditions. Bull Bayou consisted primarily of sunfish species (Centrarchidae, 51.5%) with 32.7% of the community being Longear sunfish (*Lepomis megalotis*), a species moderately tolerant to poor water quality (Tables 1 and 2). Darter species that are typically sensitive to human disturbance were the second most abundant at 33.9% of the community, of which Orangebelly darters made up 26.7% of the community. Gulpha Creek rated as having fair (IBI score of 20) stream integrity, while Bull Bayou rated as good (IBI score of 28) due to higher species richness, number of sensitive species, percentage of top carnivores and no occurrence of disease (Table 3).

Table 1. Number of species, diversity, and percent composition of sucker, sunfish, and darter/sculpin/madtom species for reaches sampled at HOSP, 2009.

Fish Parameter	Gulpha Creek	Bull Bayou
Species Richness	7	17
Simpson's Diversity	0.20	0.20
Catch Per Unit of Effort (catch/min)	1.8	2.9
Sucker Species		
Number of species	0	1
% Composition	0	0.6
Sunfish Species		
Number of species	3	4
% Composition of all sunfish	21.7	51.5
% Composition excluding tolerant species	15.9	32.7
Darter, Sculpin, Madtom Species		
Number of species	1	4
% Composition	29.0	34.5

Table 2. Number of fish caught from reaches sampled at HOSP, 2009. An asterisk indicates species sensitive to human disturbance and poor water quality.

Family	Common Name	Scientific Name	Number Caught
Gulpha Creek			
Centrarchidae	Longear sunfish	*Lepomis megalotis*	11
Centrarchidae	Green sunfish	*Lepomis cyanellus*	3
Centrarchidae	Bluegill	*Lepomis macrochirus*	1
Cyprinidae	Striped shiner*	*Luxilus chrysocephalus*	6
Cyprinidae	Creek chub	*Semotilus atromaculatus*	18
Cyprinidae	Central stoneroller	*Campostoma anomalum*	10
Percidae	Orangebelly darter*	*Etheostoma radiosum*	20
Bull Bayou			
Catostomidae	Northern hog sucker*	*Hypentelium nigricans*	1
Centrarchidae	Longear sunfish	*Lepomis megalotis*	54
Centrarchidae	Largemouth bass	*Micropterus salmoides*	1
Centrarchidae	Bluegill	*Lepomis macrochirus*	10
Centrarchidae	Green sunfish	*Lepomis cyanellus*	20
Cyprinidae	Striped shiner*	*Luxilus chrysocephalus*	3
Cyprinidae	Central stoneroller	*Campostoma anomalum*	10
Cyprinidae	Redfin shiner	*Lythrurus umbratilis*	1
Esocidae	Grass pickerel	*Esox americanus*	1
Fundulidae	Blackspotted topminnow	*Fundulus olivaceus*	3
Ictaluridae	Yellow bullhead	*Ameiurus natalis*	2
Percidae	Greenside darter*	*Etheostoma blennioides*	6
Percidae	Logperch	*Percina caprodes*	6
Percidae	Orangebelly darter*	*Etheostoma radiosum*	44
Percidae	Ouachita madtom*	*Noturus lachneri*	1
Petromyzonidae	Larval lamprey	*Ichthyomyzon spp.*	1
Poeciliidae	Mosquitofish	*Gambusia affinis*	1

Table 3. Index of Biotic Integrity (IBI) scores and metric values for each reach sampled at HOSP, 2009.

IBI Metrics	Gulpha Creek	Bull Bayou
Species Richness and Composition		
Number of fish species	7	17
Number of Cyprinidae species	3	3
Number of sensitive species	2	5
% individuals as Green sunfish	4.3	12.1
Trophic Composition		
Ratio of generalist to specialist feeders	2.5 to 1	1.9 to 1
% individuals as top carnivores	0	1.2
Fish Abundance and Condition		
Number of individuals in sample (Catch/minute)	1.8	2.9
% individuals with disease or anomaly	1.4	0
IBI Score	20	28

Habitat and Water Quality

Bull Bayou was wider (by 40%) and deeper (by 52%) on average with a higher discharge (42%) than Gulpha Creek (Table 4). Average substrate size was large pebble/small cobble (Wentworth sizes of 15 and 16) for both streams. Fish cover was primarily small woody debris (77% of the reach) in Gulpha Creek, while Bull Bayou had primarily tree/root cover (59%) in addition to small woody debris (41%) (Figure 2). Banks at Bull Bayou were relatively stable with 91% of bank angles less than 60° and over 95% of the banks covered with at least 50% vegetation and less than 3 m in height (Table 5). Gulpha Creek had higher percentage of the banks with angles greater then 60° (50%) and bank heights greater than 3 m (32%). However, the majority of banks in this stream consisted of stable bedrock (55%, Table 5) due to the presence of bluffs (23% of the bank, Figure 2).

All water quality parameters measured in Gulpha Creek and Bull Bayou showed low variability over the 48 hour time period and were within the Arkansas Pollution Control and Ecology Commission water quality standards (APCEC 2010) for surface waters of the Ouachita Mountains (Table 6).

9

Table 4. Average width, depth, velocity, substrate ($\pm$ one standard error) and total discharge for each reach sampled at HOSP, 2009.

Habitat Parameter	Gulpha Creek	Bull Bayou
Width (m)	5.2 $\pm$ 0.3	8.6 $\pm$ 1.1
Depth (cm)	16.2 $\pm$ 1.5	34.1 $\pm$ 3.3
Velocity (m/s)	0.22 $\pm$ 0.04	0.11 $\pm$ 0.03
Substrate (Wentworth code)	16.2 $\pm$ 1.0	15.3 $\pm$ 0.9
Total Discharge (m^2/s)	0.07	0.12

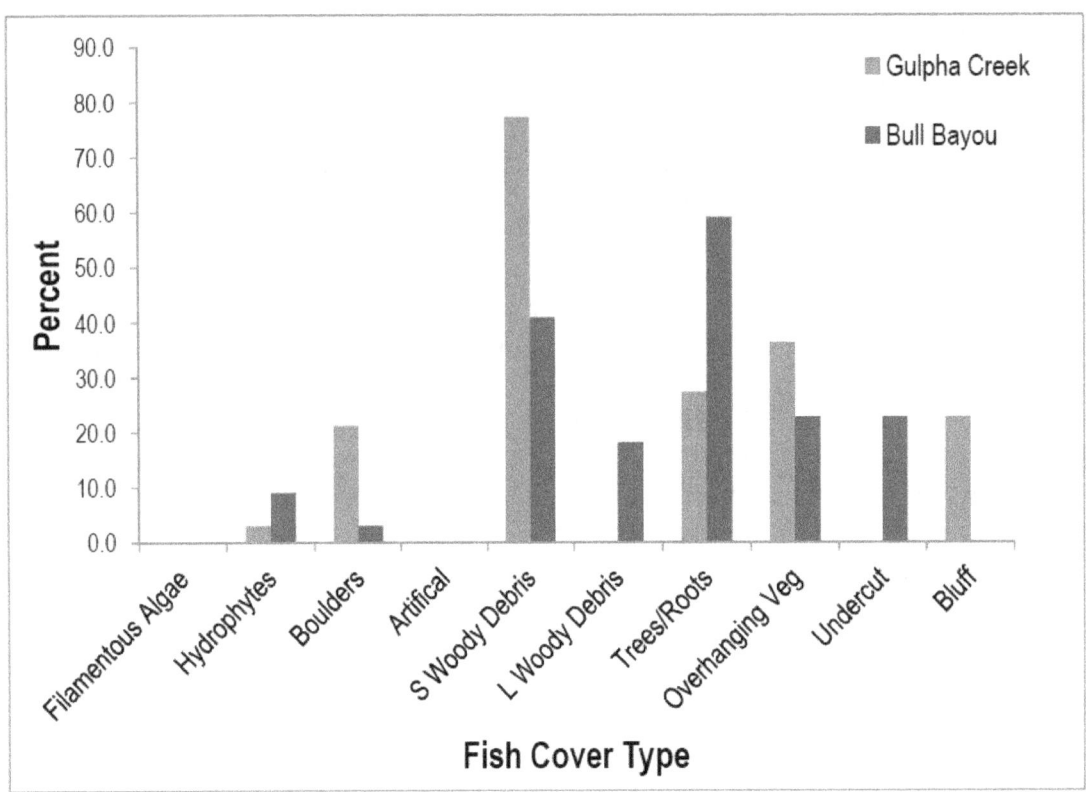

Figure 2. Percentage of the reach with individual fish cover types for each reach sampled at HOSP, 2009. Because several types of cover could be present at a transect, percentages do not add to 100%.

Table 5. Bank angle, percent vegetation, height, and substrate characteristics for each reach sampled at HOSP, 2009.

Bank Measurement	% of Total Bank	
	Gulpha Creek	Bull Bayou
Angle		
$\leq 60°$	50.0	90.9
$> 60°$	50.0	9.1
% Vegetation		
> 80%	18.2	0.0
50 - 80%	68.2	95.5
< 50%	13.6	4.5
Height		
< 1m	36.4	22.7
1 - 2m	13.6	54.5
2 - 3m	18.2	22.7
> 3m	31.8	0.0
Substrate		
Bedrock/Artificial	54.5	13.6
Boulder/Cobble	18.2	9.1
Silt	0.0	0.0
Sand	22.7	45.5
Sand/Gravel	4.5	31.8

Table 6. Average water quality parameters ($\pm$ one standard error) for each reach sampled at HOSP in 2009 and Arkansas Pollution Control and Ecology Commission water quality standards for Ouachita Mountains surface waters (APCEC 2010).

Water Quality Parameter	Gulpha Creek	Bull Bayou	APCEC (2010) Standards
Water Temperature ($°C$)	24.0 $\pm$ 0.1	24.2 $\pm$ 0.2	< 30[1]
Specific Conductance ($\mu S/cm$)	119.3 $\pm$ 0.5	60.6 $\pm$ 0.1	N/A
Dissolved Oxygen (mg/L)	7.91 $\pm$ 0.03	8.69 $\pm$ 0.07	2 - 6[2]
pH	7.69 $\pm$ 0.01	6.95 $\pm$ 0.01	6.0 - 9.0[3]
Turbidity (NTU)	0.64 $\pm$ 0.02	1.19 $\pm$ 0.05	≤ 10[4]

[1] Not to exceed 29 °C

[2] In <26.0 km^2 watersheds, minimum of 2 mg/L during critical season and 6 mg/L during primary season.

[3] Not to fluctuate > 1.0 pH unit over 24 hour period and not be < 6.0 or > 9.0.

[4] Not to exceed 10.0 ntu during baseflows.

Discussion

Although the park lies adjacent to the city of Hot Springs, the fish community of both Gulpha Creek and Bull Bayou had good diversity, fair/good stream integrity, and sensitive species. However, Bull Bayou had higher species richness, IBI score (stream integrity), and number of intolerant species which included the Ouachita madtom (*Noturus lachneri*), an Arkansas species of greatest conservation concern (Anderson 2006). Bull Bayou also had no incidence of disease or anomalies, indicating that this stream may be in better condition than Gulpha Creek which has major roadways that lie along and cross the creek in several locations.

In July and October 2003, Petersen and Justus (2005) sampled a site on Bull Bayou and on Gulpha Creek which correspond closely to our sample sites. They collected a similar number of species from these streams: 19 species from Bull Bayou (July 2003) and 11 species at the upstream campground site on Gulpha Creek (October 2003). At Bull Bayou, 13 species were in common between our 2009 sample and the 2003 sample with all five intolerant taxa present during both sample dates. Six species not found in 2009 were collected in 2003, and four species were collected in 2009, but were not found in 2003. These ten species were all rare (<2%) in the samples and likely have a patchy distribution in the stream. All seven species we collected at Gulpha Creek were also found in the 2003 sample, but Petersen and Justus also collected Largemouth bass (*Micropterus salmoides*) and Northern hog sucker (*Hypentelium nigricans*), indicating that larger bodied species and top carnivores do utilize Gulpha Creek during times of the year (October) that were not sampled during our monitoring (June).

Water quality parameters measured during our monitoring were found to be within the standards set by the state of Arkansas (APCEC 2010). However, our water quality analysis was limited to five parameters, and we did not collect other water chemistry variables related to urbanization that may be harmful to fishes and other aquatic organisms. Both streams had sufficient in-stream and bank fish cover and relatively stable banks. In summary, the portions of Bull Bayou and Gulpha Creek located within HOSP provides good habitat for a healthy native fish community typical of wadeable Ouachita Mountain streams.

Literature Cited

Anderson, J.E. (Ed) 2006. Arkansas Wildlife Action Plan. Arkansas Game and Fish Commission, Little Rock, Arkansas.

Arkansas Pollution Control and Ecology Commission (APCEC). 2010. Regulation No. 2, As Amended Regulation Establishing Water Quality Standard for Surface Waters of the State of Arkansas. Arkansas Pollution Control and Ecology Commission Report. Arkansas Pollution Control and Ecology Commission, Little Rock, Arkansas.

Barbour, M. T., J. Gerritsen, B. D. Snyder, and J. B. Stribling. 1999. Rapid bioassessment protocols for use in streams and wadeable rivers: periphyton, benthic macroinvertebrate, and fish, 2nd edition. EPA 841-B-99-002, U.S. Environmental Protection Agency, Washington, DC.

Dauwalter, D. C., E. J. Pert, and W. E. Keith. 2003. An index of biotic integrity for fish assemblages in Ozark Highland Streams of Arkansas. *Southeastern Naturalist* 2:447-468.

Dodd, H. R., D. G. Peitz, G. A. Rowell, D. E. Bowles, and L. M. Morrison. 2008. Protocol for monitoring fish communities in small streams in the Heartland Inventory and Monitoring Network. Natural Resource Report NPS/HTLN/NRR—2008/052. National Park Service, Fort Collins, Colorado.

Hlass, L. J., W. L. Fisher, D. J. Turton. 1998. Use of the index of biotic integrity to assess water quality in forested streams of the Ouachita Mountains Ecoregion, Arkansas. *Journal of Freshwater Ecology* 13:181-192.

Karr J. R. 1981. Assessment of biotic integrity using fish communities. *Fisheries* 6:21–27.

Lazorchak, J. M., Klemm, D. J., and D. V. Peck. 1998. Environmental monitoring and assessment program-surface waters: field operations and methods for measuring the ecological condition of wadeable streams. EPA/620/R-94/004F. U.S. Environmental Protection Agency, Washington, DC.

Moulton, S. R. III, J. G. Kennen, R. M. Goldstein, and J. A. Hambrook. 2002. Revised protocols for sampling algal, invertebrate, and fish communities as part of the National Water-Quality Assessment Program. U.S. Geological Survey, Reston, Virginia. Open-file Report 02-150.

Petersen, J.C. and B.G. Justus. 2005. The fishes of Hot Springs National Park, Arkansas, 2003. U.S. Geological Survey, Reston, Virginia. Scientific Investigations Report 2005-5126.

Pflieger, W. L. 1997. The fishes of Missouri. Missouri Department of Conservation, Jefferson City, Missouri.

Robison, H. W., and T. M. Buchanan. 1988. Fishes of Arkansas. University of Arkansas Press, Fayetteville, AR.

Smogor, R. 2005. Draft manual for interpreting Illinois fish IBI scores. Illinois Environmental Protection Agency, Bureau of Water, Surface Water Section.